Scrum:
a Breathtakingly Brief and Agile Introduction

This overview of roles, artifacts and the sprint cycle is adapted from

The Elements of Scrum

by Chris Sims & Hillary Louise Johnson

Scrum: a Breathtakingly Brief
and Agile Introduction
©2012 Chris Sims & Hillary Louise Johnson
ISBN # 978-1-937965-04-4

Published by Dymaxicon
An Imprint of Agile Learning Labs

Material in this book has been adapted from
The Elements of Scrum by Chris Sims & Hillary
Louise Johnson

Contents

What is Scrum?

Scrum is a lightweight framework designed to help small, close-knit teams of people develop complex products. The brainchild of a handful of software engineers working together in the late 20th Century, scrum has gained the most traction in the technology sector, but it is not inherently technical and you can easily adapt the tools and practices described in this book to other industries. You can use scrum to build a better mousetrap, for example, or to run the marketing division of a puppy chow company. You can even use it to collaborate on writing a book—we did.

A scrum team typically consists of around seven people who work together in short, sustainable bursts of activity called sprints, with plenty of time for review and reflection built in. One of the mantras of scrum is "inspect and adapt," and scrum teams are characterized by an intense focus on continuous improvement—of their process, but also of the product.

This tiny book is a just-the-facts-ma'am introduction to the various moving parts of scrum: the various roles, artifacts and events that occupy the sprint cycle.

Start
with a
bright
idea!

form a scrum team:
- product owner
- scrum master
- team members

Create
a
product
backlog...

Roles

*Scrum recognizes only
three distinct roles:
product owner,
scrum master,
and team member*

Product Owner

A development team represents a significant investment on the part of the business. There are salaries to pay, offices to rent, computers and software to buy and maintain and on and on. The product owner is responsible for maximizing the return the business gets on this investment (ROI).

One way that the product owner maximizes ROI is by directing the team toward the most valuable work, and away from less valuable work. That is, the product owner controls the order, sometimes called priority, of items in the team's backlog. In scrum, no-one but the product owner is authorized to ask the team to do work or to change the order of backlog items.

Another way that the product owner maximizes the value realized from the team's efforts is to make sure the team fully understands the requirements. If the team fully understands the requirements, then they will build the right thing, and not waste time building the wrong thing. The product owner is responsible for recording the requirements, often in the form of user stories (eg, "As a <role>, I want <a feature>, so that I can <accomplish something>") and adding them to the product backlog. Each of these users stories, when completed, will incrementally increase in the value of the product. For this reason, we often say that each time a user story is done we have a new product increment.

As a <type of user>,
I want to <do something>,
so that <some value is created>.

The Product Owner Role in a Nutshell:

* holds the vision for the product
* represents the interests of the business
* represents the customers
* owns the product backlog
* orders (prioritizes) the items in the product backlog
* creates acceptance criteria for the backlog items
* is available to answer team members' questions

Scrum Master

The scrum master acts as a coach, guiding the team to ever-higher levels of cohesiveness, self-organization, and performance. While a team's deliverable is the product, a scrum master's deliverable is a high-performing, self-organizing team.

The scrum master is the team's good shepherd, its champion, guardian, facilitator, and scrum expert. The scrum master helps the team learn and apply scrum and related agile practices to the team's best advantage. The scrum master is constantly available to the team to help them remove any impediments or road-blocks that are keeping them from doing their work. The scrum master is not—we repeat, not—the team's boss. This is a peer position on the team, set apart by knowledge and responsibilities not rank.

The scrum master role in a Nutshell:

* scrum expert and advisor
* coach
* impediment bulldozer
* facilitator

Team Member

High-performing scrum teams are highly collaborative; they are also self-organizing. The team members doing the work have total authority over how the work gets done. The team alone decides which tools and techniques to use, and which team members will work on which tasks. The theory is that the people who do the work are the highest authorities on how best to do it. Similarly, if the business needs schedule estimates, it is the team members who should create these estimates.

A scrum team should posess all of the skills required to create a potentially shippable product. Most often, this means we will have a team of specialists, each with their own skills to contribute to the team's success. However, on a scrum team, each team member's role is not to simply contribute in their special area. The role of each and every team member is to help the team deliver potentially shippable product in each sprint. Often, the best way for a team member to do this is by contributing work in their area of specialty. Other times, however, the team will need them to work outside their area of specialty in order to best move backlog items (aka user stories) from "in progress" to "done." What we are describing is a mindset change from "doing my job" to "doing the job." It is also a change in focus from "what we are doing" (work) to what is getting done (results).

The Team Member Role in a Nutshell:

* responsible for completing user stories to incrementally increase the value of the product
* self-organizes to get all of the necessary work done
* creates and owns the estimates
* owns the " how to do the work" decisions
* avoids siloed "not my job" thinking

7 +/- 2

So, how many team members should a scrum team have? The common rule of thumb is seven, plus or minus two. That is, from five to nine. Fewer team members and the team may not have enough variety of skills to do all of the work needed to complete user stories. More team members and the communication overhead starts to get excessive.

Scrum Artifacts

These are the tools we scrum practitioners use to make our process visible.

The Product Backlog

The product backlog is the cumulative list of desired deliverables for the product. This includes features, bug fixes, documentation changes, and anything else that might be meaningful and valuable to produce. Generically, they are all referred to as "backlog items." While backlog item is technically correct, many scrum teams prefer the term "user story," as it reminds us that we build products to satisfy our users' needs.

The list of user stories is ordered such that the most important story, the one that the team should do next, is at the top of the list. Right below it is the story that the team should do second, and so on. Since stories near the top of the product backlog will be worked on soon, they should be small and well understood by the whole team. Stories further down in the list can be larger and less well understood, as it will be some time before the team works on them.

Each item, or story, in the product backlog should include the following information:

* Which users the story will benefit (who it is for)
* A brief description of the desired functionality (what needs to be built)
* The reason that this story is valuable (why we should do it)
* An estimate as to how much work the story requires to implement
* Acceptance criteria that will help us know when it has been implemented correctly

The Sprint Backlog

The sprint backlog is the team's to do list for the sprint. Unlike the product backlog, it has a finite life-span: the length of the current sprint. It includes: all the stories that the team has committed to delivering this sprint and their associated tasks. Stories are deliverables, and can be thought of as units of value. Tasks are things that must be done, in order to deliver the stories, and so tasks can be thought of as units of work. A story is something a team delivers; a task is a bit of work that a person does. Each story will normally require many tasks.

Burn Charts

A burn chart shows us the relationship between time and scope. Time is on the horizontal X-axis and scope is on the vertical Y-axis. A burn up chart shows us how much scope the team has got done over a period of time. Each time something new is completed the line on the chart moves up. A burn down chart shows us what is left to do. In general, we expect the work remaining to go down over time as the team gets things done. Sometimes the work remaining changes suddenly, when scope is added or removed. These events appear as vertical lines on the burn down chart: a vertical line up when we add new work, or down when we remove some work from the plan.

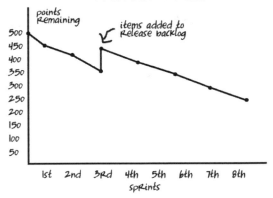

Release BuRn Down ChaRt

Task Board

When the team's tasks are visible to everyone from across the room, you never have to worry that some important piece of work will be forgotten.

The simplest task board consists of three columns: to do, doing and done. Tasks move across the board, providing visibility regarding which tasks are done, which are in progress, and which are yet to be started. This visibility helps the team inspect their current situation and adapt as needed. The board also helps stakeholders see the progress that the team is making.

Task Board

To Do	Doing	Done

Definition of Done

Done is a wonderful word; when the team gets a user story done it's time to celebrate! But sometimes there is confusion about exactly what that word "done" means. A programmer might call something done when the code has been written. The tester might think that done means that all of the tests have passed. The operations person might think that done means it's been loaded onto the production servers. A business person may think that done means we can now sell it to customers, and it's ready for them to use. This confusion about what "done" means can cause plenty of confusion and trouble, when the salesperson asks why the team is still working on the same story that the programmer said was done two weeks ago!

In order to avoid confusion, good scrum teams create their own definition of the word "done" when it is applied to a user story. They decide together what things will be complete before the team declares a story to be done. The team's definition may include things like: code written, code reviewed, unit tests passing, regression tests passing, documentation written, product owner sign-off, and so on. This list of things that the team agrees to always do before declaring a story done becomes the teams "definition of done." The team will likely print out their definition of done as a checklist, and post it next to their task board. When the team thinks a story is done, they all gather around and review each item, to confirm that it has been completed. Only then will the team declare the story as done.

daily scrum
inspect + adapt
for the sprint

sprint backlog

stories

tasks

sprint planning:
what & how

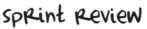

SPRINT REVIEW
inspect + adapt
for the product

RETROSPECTIVE
inspect + adapt
for the team

story time

The Sprint Cycle

The sprint cycle consists of several meetings, often called ceremonies:
sprint planning
daily scrum
story time
sprint review
retrospective

It's about rhythm

The sprint cycle is the foundational rhythm of the scrum process. Whether you call your development period a sprint, a cycle or an iteration, you are talking about exactly the same thing: a fixed period of time within which you bite off small bits of your project and finish them before returning to bite off a few more. At the end of your sprint, you will be demonstrating working software or thy name is Mud.

The more frequently the team delivers a potentially shippable product increment, the greater freedom the business has in deciding when and what to ship. Notice that there are 2 separate decisions here:

Is the product potentially shippable? That is to say, is the quality high enough that the business could ship it? Are all of the current stories done? This is a decision for the team.

Does it make business sense to ship what we have at this time? Is there enough incremental value present to take the current product to market? This is a decision for the business.

Additionally, the more frequently the team delivers and demonstrates a potentially shippable product increment, the more frequently the team gets feedback, which fuels the important inspect-and-adapt cycle. The shorter the sprint cycle, the more frequently the team is delivering value to the business.

As of this writing, it is common for scrum teams to work in sprints that last two weeks, and many teams are starting to work in one-week sprints. Much of the original writing about scrum assumed a month-long sprint, and at the time that seemed very short indeed!

The table that follows maps out the various meetings you would schedule during a one-week sprint. You don't have to call them meetings if you're allergic to the term or consider meetings to be a form of repetitive stress injury; you can call them ceremonies, as many scrum adherents do. The meeting lengths shown are an appropriate starting point for a team doing one-week sprints.

Daily Schedule for a One-Week Sprint

MONDAY	TUESDAY	WEDNESDAY	THURSDAY	FRIDAY
	STAND-UP 15 min.	STAND-UP 15 min.	STAND-UP 15 min.	STAND-UP 15 min.
SPRINT PLANNING 2 HRS.				
				SPRINT REVIEW 1/2 HR.
		STORY TIME 1 HR.		RETROSPECTIVE 90 minutes

Sprint Planning Meeting

Sprint planning marks the beginning of the sprint. Commonly, this meeting has two parts. The goal of the first part is for the team to commit to a set of deliverables for the sprint. During the second part of the meeting, the team identifies the tasks that must be completed in order to deliver the agreed upon user stories. We recommend one to two hours of sprint planning per week of development.

Part One: "What will we do?"

The goal of part one of the sprint planning meeting is to emerge with a set of "committed" stories that the whole team believes they can deliver by the end of the sprint. The product owner leads this part of the meeting.

  One by one, in priority order, the product owner presents the stories he would like the team to complete during this sprint. As each story is presented, the team members discuss it with the product owner and review acceptance criteria to make sure they have a common understanding of what is expected. Then the team members decide if they can commit to delivering that story by the end of the sprint. This process repeats for each story, until the team feels that they can't commit to any more work. Note the separation in authority: the product owner decides which stories will be considered, but the team members doing the actual work are the ones who decide how much work they can take on.

Part 2: "How will we do it?"

In phase two of the sprint planning meeting, the team rolls up its sleeves and begins to decompose the selected stories into tasks. Remember that stories are deliverables: things that stakeholders, users, and customers want. In order to deliver a story, team members will have to complete tasks. Task are things like: get additional input from users; design a new screen; add new columns to the database; do black-box testing of the new feature; write help text; get the menu items translated for our target locales; run the release scripts.

The product owner should be available during this half of the meeting to answer questions. The team may also need to adjust the list of stories it is committing to, as during the process of identifying tasks the team members may realize that they have signed up for too many or too few stories.

The output of the sprint planning meeting is the sprint backlog, the list of all the committed stories, with their associated tasks. The product owner agrees not to ask for additional stories during the sprint, unless the team specifically asks for more. The product owner also commits to being available to answer questions about the stories, negotiate their scope, and provide product guidance until the stories are acceptable and can be considered done.

Daily Scrum

The daily scrum, sometimes called the stand-up meeting, is:

Daily. Most teams choose to hold this meeting at the start of their work day. You can adapt this to suit your team's preferences.

Brief. The point of standing up is to discourage the kinds of tangents and discursions that make for meeting hell. The daily scrum should always be held to no more than 15 minutes.

Pointed. Each participant quickly shares:

* What tasks I've completed since the last daily scrum.
* What tasks I expect to complete by the next daily scrum.
* What obstacles are slowing me down.

The goal of this meeting is to inspect and adapt the work the team members are doing, in order to successfully complete the stories that the team has committed to deliver. The inspection happens in the meeting; the adaptation may happen after the meeting. This means that the team needn't solve problems in the meeting: simply surfacing the issues and deciding which team members will address them is usually sufficient. Remember, this meeting is brief!

Story Time

In this meeting you will be discussing and improving the stories in your product backlog, which contains all the stories for future sprints. Note that these are not the stories in the current sprint--those stories are now in the sprint backlog. We recommend one hour per week, every week, regardless of the length of your sprint. In this meeting, the team works with the product owner to:

Define and Refine Acceptance Criteria

Each user story in the product backlog should include a list of acceptance criteria. These are pass/fail testable conditions that help us know when then the story is implemented as intended. Some people like to think of them as acceptance examples: the examples that the team will demonstrate to show that the story is done.

Story Sizing (Estimation)

During story time, the team will assign a size (estimate, if you prefer that term) to stories that haven't yet been sized. This is the team's guess at how much work will be required to get the story completely done.

<- smallest   largest ->

☐☐ ☐ ☐ ☐ ☐ ☐☐ ☐☐ ☐☐

Story Splitting

Stories at the top of the product backlog need to be small. Small stories are easier for everyone to understand, and easier for the team to complete in a short period of time. Stories further down in the product backlog can be larger and less well defined. This implies that we need to break the big stories into smaller stories as they make their way up the list. While the product owner may do much of this work on their own, story time is their chance to get help from the whole team.

As of this writing, the story time meeting isn't an "official" scrum meeting. We suspect it will be in the future, as all of the high performing scrum teams we know use the story time meeting to help keep their product backlog groomed.

Sprint Review

This is the public end of the sprint; invite any and all stakeholders to this meeting. It's the team's chance to show off its accomplishments, the stories that have met the team's definition of done. This is also the stakeholders' opportunity to see how the product has been incrementally improved over the course of the sprint.

If there are stories that the team committed to but did not complete, this is the time to share that information with the stakeholders. Then comes the main event of this meeting: demonstrating the stories that did get done. Undoubtedly the stakeholders will have feedback and ideas, and the product owner and the team members will gather this feedback, which will help the team to inspect-and-adapt the product.

This meeting is not a decision-making meeting. It's not when we decide if the stories are done; that must happen before this meeting. It's not when we make decisions or commitments about what the team will do during the next sprint; that happens in sprint planning.

How long should the sprint review be? We recommend scheduling one-half to one hour for every week of development. That is, if you have a one-week sprint, then this meeting might be 30 to 60 minutes. If you have a two-week sprint, then this meeting might need one to two hours. After you have done it a few times, you will know how long your team needs—inspect and adapt!

Retrospective

While the sprint review is the public end of the sprint, the team has one more meeting: the retrospective. Scrum is designed to help teams continuously inspect and adapt, resulting in ever-improving performance and happiness. The retrospective, held at the very end of each and every sprint, is dedicated time for the team to focus on what was learned during the sprint, and how that learning can be applied to make some improvement. We recommend one to two hours of retrospective time for each week of development.

Unlike the traditional "post mortem," the aim of a retrospective is never to generate a long laundry list of things that went well and things that went wrong, but to identify no more than one or two strategic changes to make in the next sprint. It's about process improvement.

Abnormal Sprint Termination (When Good Sprints Go Bad)

In scrum, the basic agreement between management and the team is that management won't change up requirements during a sprint. Still, every once in a while something happens that invalidates everything in the sprint plan—a business is sold, a game-changing technology enters the market, a competitor makes a move. The decision to terminate the sprint early is fundamentally a business decision, so the product owner gets to make the call on an "abnormal sprint termination." Despite the name, neither Arnold Schwarzenegger nor James Cameron need get involved.

If the product owner does decide to terminate the sprint early, the team will back out any changes that they have made during the sprint to avoid the problems that come from half-done work. Holding a retrospective is especially important after a sprint is abnormally terminated, as it helps the team learn from the experience.

Inspect & Adapt, Baby!

So, why do we do development work in these short cycles? To learn. Experience is the best teacher, and the scrum cycle is designed to provide you with multiple opportunities to receive feedback—from customers, from the team, from the market—and to learn from it. What you learn while doing the work in one cycle informs your planning for the next cycle. In scrum, we call this "inspect and adapt"; you might call it "continuous improvement"; either way, it's a beautiful thing.

That's it!
Ready,
set,
sprint!

Appendix:
Values & Principles

The values and principles outlined in the Agile Manifesto, while not a part of scrum framework, served to inform the creators of scrum and provide a lot of context for understanding the why of scrum. We didn't write them, but we're including them here in their entirety for your edification and enjoyment.

Agile Principles

Our highest priority is to satisfy the customer
through early and continuous delivery
of valuable software.

Welcome changing requirements, even late in
development. Agile processes harness change for
the customer's competitive advantage.

Deliver working software frequently, from a
couple of weeks to a couple of months, with a
preference to the shorter timescale.

Business people and developers must work
together daily throughout the project.

Build projects around motivated individuals.
Give them the environment and support they need,
and trust them to get the job done.

The most efficient and effective method of
conveying information to and within a development
team is face-to-face conversation.

Working software is the primary measure of progress.

Agile processes promote sustainable development.
The sponsors, developers, and users should be able
to maintain a constant pace indefinitely.

Continuous attention to technical excellence
and good design enhances agility.

Simplicity--the art of maximizing the amount
of work not done--is essential.

The best architectures, requirements, and designs
emerge from self-organizing teams.

At regular intervals, the team reflects on how
to become more effective, then tunes and adjusts
its behavior accordingly.

Agile Values

Individuals and interactions over processes and tools
Working software over comprehensive documentation
Customer collaboration over contract negotiation
Responding to change over following a plan

Source: agilemanifesto.org

About the Authors

Chris Sims is a Certified Scrum Trainer and agile coach who has been helping teams improve their happiness and productivity since the turn of the century. He has made a living in roles such as: scrum master, product owner, engineering manager, C++ developer, musician, and auto mechanic. Chris is the founder of Agile Learning Labs and a frequent presenter at agile conferences.

Hillary Louise Johnson is an author and former business journalist who has written on innovation, technology and pop culture for *Inc* magazine and the *Los Angeles Times*. As an intellectual property consultant she has drafted numerous technology patents. She has been editor-in-chief of several print and online publications and is now Agile Learning Labs' creative director.

Love it? Hate it?
Review it!

Amazon reviews help other readers like you discover books, so whether you adored this book or loathed it to pieces, we urge you to take a few moments to share your sentiments at amazon.com.

If you enjoyed this title...

...you can learn even more from *The Elements of Scrum*. Peppered with anecdotes, illustrations and all of the supporting practices you'll need to be agile, *The Elements of Scrum* has helped thousands of readers become happier and more productive. Here is what some of our Amazon readers have said about *Elements*:

"If you want to understand the essentials of Agile development and Scrum, The Elements of Scrum *by Chris Sims and Hillary Louise Johnson is a must read."* -Dave Moran

"Bravo. 6 stars. I wish all computer books were written like this." -T. McCann

"As a consultant who works in agile, this is the book I've been waiting for." -Liz Lewison

"For those only dancing with the idea of learning scrum and agile, I have three words—Read this Book." -Brendan Kane

You'll find **The Elements of Scrum** on Amazon for $29.95 trade paperback, $9.99 Kindle.

Made in the USA
San Bernardino, CA
22 December 2014